D1569980

A JARROLD COMPANION

Words of Friendship

WORDS OF FRIENDSHIP

No man is useless while he has a friend.
ROBERT LOUIS STEVENSON

❦

*All his faults are such that one loves him
still the better for them.*
OLIVER GOLDSMITH

❦

*Many a friendship, long, loyal,
and self-sacrificing, rested at first on no thicker
foundation than a kind word.*
FREDERICK F. FABER

❦

*Friends need not agree in everything or go
always together, or have no comparable other
friendship of the same intimacy. On the contrary, in
friendship union is more about ideal things.*
GEORGE SANTAYANA

WORDS OF FRIENDSHIP

The friends of my friends are my friends.
A FRENCH PROVERB

❧

Caring is everything, nothing matters but caring.
BARON FRIEDRICH VON HUGEL

❧

*It is always safe to learn, even from our enemies –
seldom safe to instruct, even our friends.*
CHARLES CALEB COLTON

❧

*The finest kind of friendship is between
people who expect a great deal from each other
but never ask it.*

❧

He makes no friends who never made a foe.
ALFRED, LORD TENNYSON

WORDS OF FRIENDSHIP

Friendships multiply joys and divide griefs.
H.C. BOHN

❧

The road to a friend's house is never long.

❧

*The essence of true friendship
is to make allowance for another's little lapses.*
DAVID STOREY

❧

*The privilege of a special friend
is that they never require an explanation.*

❧

*One can never speak enough of the virtues,
the dangers, the power of shared laughter.*
FRANÇOISE SAGAN

WORDS OF FRIENDSHIP

When we truly care for ourselves,
it becomes possible to care far more profoundly
about other people. The more alert and sensitive we
are to our own needs, then the more loving and
generous we can be toward others.

EDA LeSHAN

It seems to me that the one privilege
of friendship is to make the best of friends,
to encourage and believe in them,
to hand on the pleasant things.

A.C. BENSON

I am learning to live close to the lives
of my friends without ever seeing them.
No miles of any measurement can separate
your soul from mine.

JOHN MUIR

WORDS OF FRIENDSHIP

*Friendship is a union of spirits,
a marriage of hearts.*
WILLIAM PENN

*I'm telling you it's odd but true,
The richest folk are not
The ones who always like to boast
About the wealth they've got.
The rich are kindly folk who smile,
And warm our hearts a little while.*

*Friends are an aid to the young,
to guard them from error; to the elderly,
to attend to their wants and to supplement their
failing power of action; to those in the prime
of life, to assist them to noble deeds.*
ARISTOTLE

WORDS OF FRIENDSHIP

*You may light another's candle
from your own, without loss.*
PROVERB

❧

*Have you noticed how troubles seem less
when you have a friend to confide in?*

❧

A constant friend is a thing rare and hard to find.
PLUTARCH

❧

*Have friends not for the sake of receiving,
but of giving.*

❧

Fate makes our relatives, choice makes our friends.
JACQUES DELILLE

WORDS OF FRIENDSHIP

When our friends are present,
we ought to treat them well; and when they
are absent, to speak of them well.
EPICTETUS

Since there is nothing so well worth having
as friends, never lose a chance to make them.
For men are brought into constant contact with one
another, and friends help...at times and places
where you least expect it.
FRANCESCO GUICCIARDINI

From quiet homes and first beginning,
Out to the undiscovered ends,
There's nothing worth the wear of winning,
But laughter and the love of friends.
HILAIRE BELLOC

WORDS OF FRIENDSHIP

*The worst solitude is to be destitute
of sincere friendship.*
FRANCIS BACON

*My friends have made the story of my life.
In a thousand ways they have turned my
limitations into beautiful privileges, and enabled
me to walk serene and happy...*
HELEN KELLER

*True friendship is like sound health,
the value of it is seldom known until it be lost.*
CHARLES CALEB COLTON

*Complete unity of aim is the traditional
condition of genuine and sincere friendship.*
CICERO

WORDS OF FRIENDSHIP

There are moments in life when all that we can bear is the sense that our friend is near us.
HONORE DE BALZAC

❧

Neither can any man live happily who has regard to himself alone…thou must live for thy neighbour if thou wouldst live for thyself.
SENECA

❧

The ornament of a house is the friends who frequent it.
RALPH WALDO EMERSON

❧

My feeling is that there is nothing in life but refraining from hurting others, and comforting those that are sad.
OLIVE SCHREINER

WORDS OF FRIENDSHIP

Make peace with men and quarrel with your faults.
RUSSIAN PROVERB

Kindness in a friend
is more important than perfection.

We should behave to our friends
as we would wish our friends to behave to us.
ARISTOTLE

There is nothing final between friends.
WILLIAM JENNINGS BRYAN

Friends, though absent, are still present.
CICERO

WORDS OF FRIENDSHIP

*No matter what looms ahead, if you
can eat today, enjoy the sunlight today, mix good
cheer with good friends today – enjoy it
and bless God for it.*
HENRY WARD BEECHER

*No medicine is more valuable, none more
efficacious, none better suited to the cure of all our
temporal ills than a friend, to whom we may turn
for consolation in time of trouble, and with whom
we may share our happiness in time of joy.*
SAINT AILRED OF RIEVAULX

*Yes, we must ever be friends;
and of all who offer you friendship
Let me be ever the first, the truest,
the nearest and the dearest!*
HENRY WADSWORTH LONGFELLOW

WORDS OF FRIENDSHIP

Of all the means to insure happiness throughout the whole of life by far the most important is the acquisition of friends.
EPICURUS

But every road is rough to me that has no friend to cheer it.
ELIZABETH SHANE

I like a highland friend who will stand by me, not only when I am in the right, but when I am a little in the wrong.
SIR WALTER SCOTT

A smiling face is the magical sunshine that creates friendship.
ALICE E. WOODS

WORDS OF FRIENDSHIP

For what do my friends stand?
Not for the clever things they say:
I do not remember them half an hour after they
are spoken. It is always the unspoken, the
unconscious, which is their reality to me.
MARK RUTHERFORD

A friend is a person who knows all about you –
and still likes you.
ELBERT HUBBARD

It was such a joy to see thee.
I wish I could tell how much thee is to my life.
I always turn to thee as a sort of rest and often
just think about thy face when I get troubled.
I am not very good at saying all I feel, but
deep down I do feel it all so much.
LADY HENRY SOMERSET

WORDS OF FRIENDSHIP

*Friends are much better tried in bad fortune
than in good.*
ARISTOTLE

*A man, Sir, should keep his friendship
in constant repair.*
SAMUEL JOHNSON
LETTER TO LORD CHESTERFIELD

*Old friends are the great blessing of one's later
years. They have the memory of the same events and
have the same mode of thinking.*
HORACE WALPOLE

*In reality, we are still children. We want
to find a playmate for our thoughts and feelings.*
WILHELM STEKHEL

WORDS OF FRIENDSHIP

A little common sense, goodwill, and a tiny dose of unselfishness could make this goodly earth into an earthly paradise.
RICHARD ADLINGTON

We had been talking as old friends should talk, about nothing, about everything.
LILIAN HELLMAN

*Ah, how good it feels!
The hand of an old friend.*
HENRY WADSWORTH LONGFELLOW

Friendships add a brighter radiance to prosperity and lighten the burden of adversity by dividing it and sharing it.
CICERO

WORDS OF FRIENDSHIP

To have a friend, be a friend.
OLD SAYING

❧

*The friends you can call upon any time
are the friends that matter.*

❧

*Nothing but heaven itself
is better than a friend who is really a friend.*
PLAUTUS

❧

*The light of friendship is like phosphorous,
seen plainly when all around is dark.*

❧

True friends are those seeking solitude together.
ABEL BONNARD

WORDS OF FRIENDSHIP

When a friend is in trouble, don't annoy him by asking if there is anything you can do. Think up something appropriate and do it.
E.W. HOWE

Friendships aren't perfect and yet they are very precious.
LETTY COTTIN POGREBIN

It is good to have a trusted, willing listener to talk to when things are not going too well.

There is a magnet in your heart that will attract true friends. That magnet is unselfishness, thinking of others first…when you learn to live for others, they will live for you.
PARAMAHANSA YOGANANDA

WORDS OF FRIENDSHIP

The firmest friendships have been formed in mutual adversity, as iron is most strongly united by the fiercest flame.
CHARLES CALEB COLTON

Our friends are the jewels in our crown of contentment.
SARAH BAN BREATHNACH

Friendship is the only cement that will ever hold the world together.
WOODROW WILSON

One is taught by experience to put a premium on those few people who can appreciate you for what you are…
GAIL GOODWIN

When men are friendly even water is sweet.
CHINESE PROVERB

❧

The words of another can be just enough
to keep one going on and trying once again.

❧

What is a friend? I will tell you.
It is a person with whom you dare to be yourself.
FRANK CRANE

❧

A smile costs less than electricity
and gives more light.

❧

What a thing friendship is, world without end!
ROBERT BROWNING

WORDS OF FRIENDSHIP

*Human beings are born into this little span
of life of which the best thing is its friendships
and intimacies.*
WILLIAM JAMES

*Promises may get friends, but it is
performance that must nurse and keep them.*
OWEN FELLTHAM

*One who'll lend as quick as borrow,
One who's the same today as tomorrow,
One who'll share my joy and sorrow,
That's what I call a friend.*

*One discovers a friend by chance, and cannot feel
regret that twenty or thirty years of life maybe have
been spent without the least knowledge of him.*
CHARLES DUDLEY WARNER

WORDS OF FRIENDSHIP

*I have learned that to have a good friend
is the purest of all God's gifts, for it
is a love that has no exchange of payment.*
FRANCES FARMER

❧

*More than kisses, letters mingle souls;
for, thus friends absent speak.*
JOHN DONNE

❧

*It is not what you give your friend,
but what you are willing to give him,
that determines the quality of friendship.*
MARY DIXON THAYER

❧

*Friendship is a word the very sight of which
in print makes the heart warm.*
AUGUSTINE BIRRELL

WORDS OF FRIENDSHIP

*Friends are people who help you be
more yourself, more the person you intended to be.*
MERLE SHAIN

❧

No receipt openeth the heart but a true friend.
FRANCIS BACON

❧

*Friendship is the great chain of human society,
and intercourse of letters is one of the chiefest links
of that chain.*
JAMES HOWELL

❧

*He who thinks he can find himself
the means of doing without others is mistaken;
But he who thinks that others cannot do without
him is still more mistaken.*
DUC DE LA ROCHFOUCAULD

*P*erhaps the most delightful friendships are those
in which there is much agreement, much disputation,
and yet more personal liking.

GEORGE ELIOT

*T*he holy passion of Friendship is of so sweet and
steady and loyal and enduring a nature that it will
last through a whole lifetime.

MARK TWAIN

*T*here is nothing we like to see so much as
the gleam of pleasure in a person's eye when he feels
that we have sympathised with him, understood
him, interested ourself in his welfare. At these
moments something fine and spiritual passes
between two friends. These moments are the
moments worth living.

DON MARQUIS

WORDS OF FRIENDSHIP

*The truth in friendship is to me
every bit as sacred as eternal marriage.*
KATHERINE MANSFIELD

*We wouldn't really like our friends to be perfect,
would we? For one thing, what would we have in
common with them?*

*Silences make the little conversations
between friends. Not the saying, but the never
needing to say, is what counts.*
MARGARET LEE LITTLE

*Friendship consists in forgetting what one gives
and remembering what one receives.*
ALEXANDRE DUMAS

ALSO IN THIS SERIES

Words of Comfort
Words of Joy
Words of Love

First Published in Great Britain in 1997 by
JARROLD PUBLISHING LTD
Whitefriars, Norwich NR3 1TR

Developed and Produced by
FOUR SEASONS PUBLISHING LTD
1 Durrington Avenue, London SW20 8NT

Text research by *Pauline Barrett*
Designed by *Judith Pedersen*
Picture research by *Vanessa Fletcher*

Printed in Dubai

ISBN 0 7117 0968 8

ACKNOWLEDGEMENTS

Four Seasons Publishing Ltd would like to thank all those
who kindly gave permission to reproduce the words and visual
material in this book; copyright holders have been identified
where possible and we apologise for any inadvertent omissions.

Front Cover: PICNIC IN MAY, *Szinyei Merse Pal* 1873
e.t. archive
Title Page and Back Cover: JEUNES FILLES AU PIANO,
Pierre Auguste Renoir 1841-1919
Fine Art Photographic Library